C000181148

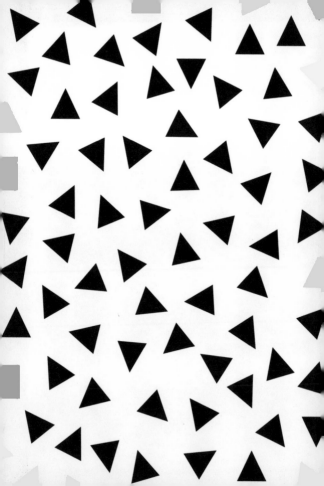

YOU
CAN
Totally
DO THIS

summersdale

YOU CAN TOTALLY DO THIS

An Hachette UK Company
www.hachette.co.uk

Summersdale Publishers Ltd
Part of Octopus Publishing Group Limited
Carmelite House
50 Victoria Embankment
LONDON
EC4Y 0DZ
UK

www.summersdale.com

Printed and bound in China

ISBN: 978-1-78783-982-3

Substantial discounts on bulk quantities of Summersdale books are available to corporations, professional associations and other organizations. For details contact general enquiries: telephone: +44 (0) 1243 771107 or email: enquiries@summersdale.com.

TO...............................

FROM...........................

AM I GOOD ENOUGH?

Yes I am.

Michelle Obama

If you don't like
something, change it.
If you can't change it,
change your attitude.

Maya Angelou

To hell with circumstances;
I create opportunities.

Bruce Lee

Your time is limited,
so don't waste it living
someone else's life.

Steve Jobs

Rise
and slay

Don't let anybody
tell you that you
can't do anything.

Tim Peake

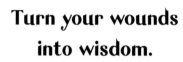

Turn your wounds
into wisdom.

Oprah Winfrey

Be a game changer

OUR GREATEST
GLORY IS NOT IN
NEVER FALLING,
BUT IN RISING
EVERY TIME
WE FALL.

Oliver Goldsmith

YOU ARE BEAUTIFUL:
EMBRACE IT.
YOU ARE INTELLIGENT:
EMBRACE IT.
YOU ARE POWERFUL:
EMBRACE IT.

MICHAELA COEL

The sun will rise in the morning.

Michael Morpurgo

THERE ARE NO REGRETS IN LIFE.
Just lessons.

Jennifer Aniston

BAD VIBES DON'T GO WITH MY OUTFIT

When the
going gets tough,
the tough reinvent.

RuPaul

When life
gives you
Monday, dip
it in glitter
and sparkle
all day.

Ella Woodward

Set your
dial to smile

*Do your thing
and don't care
if they like it.*

Tina Fey

It's always
too early to quit.

Norman Vincent Peale

So often in life, things that you regard as an impediment turn out to be great, good fortune.

Ruth Bader Ginsburg

IT DOES NOT
MATTER HOW
SLOWLY YOU GO
SO LONG AS YOU
do not stop.

Confucius

Dream big,
STAY
FOCUSED
AND MAKE
IT HAPPEN

AS ONE GOES
THROUGH LIFE,
ONE LEARNS THAT
IF YOU DON'T
PADDLE YOUR
OWN CANOE, YOU
DON'T MOVE.

Katharine Hepburn

POWER IS NOT
GIVEN TO YOU.
YOU HAVE TO
TAKE IT.

BEYONCÉ

You're not
average – you're
awesome!

Whether you believe
you can do a thing or
not, you are right.

Henry Ford

I AM DELIBERATE
AND AFRAID OF
NOTHING.

AUDRE LORDE

We always
may be what
we might
have been.

Adelaide Anne Procter

YOU MUST
EXPECT GREAT
THINGS OF
YOURSELF
BEFORE

*you can
do them.*

Michael Jordan

Be a
goal-digger

Just believe in yourself.
Even if you don't,
pretend that you do and,
at some point, you will.

Venus Williams

I choose to make the rest of my life the best of my life.

Louise Hay

ONE DAY OR DAY ONE –
you choose

BEWARE; FOR I
AM FEARLESS,
AND THEREFORE
POWERFUL.

Mary Shelley

YOU'VE GOT TO GET OUT THERE AND MAKE IT HAPPEN YOURSELF.

DIANA ROSS

Pour yourself a drink,
put on some lipstick, and
pull yourself together.

Elizabeth Taylor

Shoot for the moon.
Even if you miss, you'll
land among the stars.

Les Brown

You are
killing it!

We know
what we are,
but know not
what we
may be.

William Shakespeare

Your victory is right around the corner. Never give up.

Nicki Minaj

TAKE THE
RISK OR
LOSE THE
CHANCE

Only those who will
risk going too far can
possibly find out how
far one can go.

T. S. Eliot

You make
your own luck.

Ernest Hemingway

FORTUNE

FAVOURS

THE BOLD.

VIRGIL

It's not
the absence
of fear; it's
overcoming
it.

Emma Watson

Trust in
the process

It's amazing what you can
get if you quietly, clearly,
and authoritatively
demand it.

Meryl Streep

Impossible is just an opinion.

Paulo Coelho

IT DOESN'T
MATTER THAT
YOU FELL;
IT MATTERS
THAT YOU
GOT
back up

Winners never quit
and quitters never win.

Vince Lombardi

I've never underestimated myself. There's nothing wrong with being ambitious.

Angela Merkel

Life is about being positive
and hopeful, choosing to
be joyful, choosing to be
encouraging, choosing
to be empowering.

Billy Porter

TOMORROW BELONGS ONLY TO THE PEOPLE WHO PREPARE FOR IT TODAY.

MALCOLM X

Your
potential is
endless

The hard days
are what make
you stronger.

Aly Raisman

We were scared,
but our fear was
not as strong as
our courage.

Malala Yousafzai

YOU HAVE
ALREADY
SURVIVED
100 PER
CENT
OF YOUR
WORST
DAYS

DON'T SETTLE FOR WHAT LIFE GIVES YOU; MAKE LIFE BETTER AND *build something.*

Ashton Kutcher

I ATTRIBUTE MY SUCCESS TO THIS —
I NEVER GAVE OR TOOK AN EXCUSE.

FLORENCE NIGHTINGALE

It always seems impossible until it's done.

Anonymous

Better to live one year as a tiger, than a hundred as a sheep.

Madonna

BE
STRONGER
THAN YOUR
EXCUSES

You are beautiful and
you can do anything.

Lizzo

Always go with your passions. Never ask yourself if it's realistic or not.

Deepak Chopra

Radiate
confidence

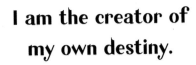

I am the creator of
my own destiny.

Alicia Keys

I am not lucky. You know what I am? I am smart, I am talented, I take advantage of the opportunities that come my way.

Shonda Rhimes

NO MATTER WHAT
HAPPENS, OR HOW
BAD IT SEEMS
TODAY, LIFE DOES
GO ON, AND
*it will be better
tomorrow.*

Maya Angelou

The only
one who can
tell you "you
can't win" is
you and you
don't have
to listen.

Jessica Ennis-Hill

Life
IS TOO
SHORT FOR
IFS, BUTS OR
MAYBES

THE MOST
DIFFICULT THING
IS THE DECISION
TO ACT. THE
REST IS MERELY
TENACITY.

Amelia Earhart

Never doubt
yourself. Never
change who
you are.

Britney Spears

Celebrate
every victory

I feel like if
it's not scaring
you, you're doing
it wrong.

Anna Kendrick

I AM NO LONGER ACCEPTING THE THINGS I CANNOT CHANGE. I AM CHANGING THE THINGS I CANNOT ACCEPT.

ANGELA DAVIS

DO NOT TWIST YOURSELF INTO SHAPES TO PLEASE.

Don't do it.

Chimamanda Ngozi Adichie

We all start somewhere. It's where you end up that counts.

Rihanna

Prove them wrong

The question isn't who's going to let me; it's who is going to stop me.

Ayn Rand

IT TAKES COURAGE TO GROW UP AND BECOME

who you really are.

E. E. Cummings

Be a
warrior, not
a worrier

If you have something you're really passionate about, don't let anyone tell you that you can't do it.

Selena Gomez

When one's mind is made up, this diminishes fear; knowing what must be done does away with fear.

Rosa Parks

None of us want
to be in calm waters
all our lives.

Jane Austen

REMAIN HUMBLE, BUT STAY HUNGRY.

CARDI B

GET OUT THERE AND CARPE THAT DIEM!

IT IS NOT THE
MOUNTAIN WE
CONQUER, BUT
OURSELVES.

Edmund Hillary

Do one thing every day that scares you.

Mary Schmich

Be you,
do you,
for you

No matter
where you're from,
your dreams are valid.

Lupita Nyong'o

IN THE END, SOME OF YOUR GREATEST PAINS BECOME YOUR GREATEST STRENGTHS.

DREW BARRYMORE

ONCE YOU CHOOSE HOPE,

anything's possible.

Christopher Reeve

Tell me, what is it you plan to do with your one wild and precious life?

Mary Oliver

Go forth
and be fierce

LIFE IS SHORT, AND IT IS HERE

to be lived.

Kate Winslet

Goals should never be easy, they should force you to work, even if they are uncomfortable at the time.

Michael Phelps

EVERY DAY IS A NEW CHANCE TO DO SOMETHING *amazing*

IF MY MIND CAN
CONCEIVE IT,
IF MY HEART
CAN BELIEVE IT,
I KNOW I CAN
ACHIEVE IT.

Jesse Jackson

I feel like people are expecting me to fail, therefore, I expect myself to win.

Lewis Hamilton

The time to be courageous is now.

Alexandria Ocasio-Cortez

IF YOU CAN'T GO STRAIGHT AHEAD, YOU GO AROUND THE CORNER.

CHER

Write your
own destiny

Optimism is
the faith that leads
to achievement;
nothing can be done
without hope.

Helen Keller

Sometimes a loss is
the best thing that
can happen. It teaches
you what you should
have done next time.

Snoop Dogg

Don't let later
become never

The most courageous act is still to think for yourself. Aloud.

Coco Chanel

The only way of
discovering the limits of
the possible is to venture
a little way past them
into the impossible.

Arthur C. Clarke

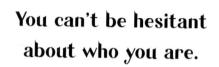

You can't be hesitant
about who you are.

Viola Davis

LIVE YOUR LIFE AS IF YOU ALREADY ARE WHERE YOU WANT TO BE.

RUSSELL SIMMONS

WAKE UP WITH
DETERMINATION
AND GO TO
BED WITH
SATISFACTION

I'm not here to be
perfect and I'm not
here to be anything
but my best, whatever
that means for me.

Jennifer Lopez

We are what
we repeatedly do.

Will Durant

WHEN YOU
FOCUS ON
THE GOOD,
THE GOOD
GETS
better

MAKE THE MOST OF YOURSELF BY FANNING THE TINY, INNER SPARKS OF POSSIBILITY INTO FLAMES OF ACHIEVEMENT.

Golda Meir

Never give
up then, for
that is just
the place and
time that the
tide'll turn.

Harriet Beecher Stowe

Accept no one's
definition of your life;
define yourself.

Harvey Fierstein

INSPIRATION IS FOR AMATEURS – THE REST OF US JUST SHOW UP AND *get to work.*

Chuck Close

Attitude is everything

IF I WAS GOING TO BE
SUCCESSFUL, I HAD
TO BE SUCCESSFUL
WITH MYSELF.

JAY-Z

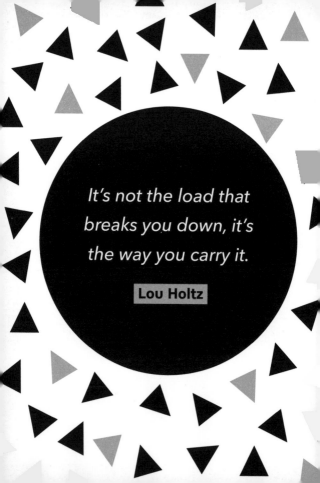

It's not the load that breaks you down, it's the way you carry it.

Lou Holtz

YOU ARE
stronger
THAN YOU
KNOW

I'm always trying
to one-up myself.

Megan Thee Stallion

HERE'S TO US BEING
AFRAID AND DOING
IT ANYWAY.

GABRIELLE UNION

Life is only about the I-tried-to-do. I don't mind the failure but I can't imagine that I'd forgive myself if I didn't try.

Nikki Giovanni

WE'RE CAPABLE
OF SO MUCH
MORE THAN WE
*allow ourselves
to believe.*

Queen Latifah

Grow through
what you go
through

When anyone
tells me
I can't do
anything...
I'm just not
listening
anymore.

Florence Griffith Joyner

Expect the unexpected. And whenever possible, be the unexpected.

Lynda Barry

PUT ON YOUR POSITIVE PANTS

I dwell in possibility.

Emily Dickinson

YOU ONLY LIVE
ONCE, BUT IF YOU
DO IT RIGHT,
once is enough.

Mae West

*Growth and comfort
do not coexist.*

Ginni Rometty

Courage doesn't always roar. Sometimes courage is the quiet voice at the end of the day saying, "I will try again tomorrow."

Mary Anne Radmacher

Embrace the unknown

The trouble is, if you don't risk anything, you risk even more.

Erica Jong

EVER TRIED.
EVER FAILED.
NO MATTER.
TRY AGAIN.
FAIL AGAIN.
FAIL BETTER.

SAMUEL BECKETT

DON'T WAIT FOR OPPORTUNITY – GO OUT AND *get it!*

When you're going to do whatever you're going to do, you have to put your mind into it.

Mary J. Blige

I never dreamed about success. I worked for it.

Estée Lauder

However
difficult
life may
seem, there
is always
something you
can do and
succeed at.

Stephen Hawking

WHY NOT GO OUT
ON A LIMB? ISN'T
THAT WHERE
THE FRUIT IS?

Frank Scully

Let success
be your noise

Embrace what makes you unique, even if it makes others uncomfortable.

Janelle Monáe

If you're walking down the right path and you're willing to keep walking, eventually you'll make progress.

Barack Obama

LIFE IS TOUGH BUT SO ARE YOU

When you come out of
the storm, you won't be
the same person who
walked in. That's what
this storm's all about.

Haruki Murakami

IT'S NEVER TOO LATE
— NEVER TOO LATE
TO START OVER,
NEVER TOO LATE
TO BE HAPPY.

JANE FONDA

If you get tired learn
to rest, not quit.

Anonymous

I have more strength
than I appear to have.

Eva Perón

Don't just
survive –
thrive

If opportunity doesn't knock, build a door.

Milton Berle

If you are
irritated by
every rub,
how will your
mirror be
polished?

Rumi

DON'T STOP
UNTIL YOU'RE
proud.

Don't allow people to dim your shine because they are blinded. Tell them to put on some sunglasses.

Lady Gaga

YOU DON'T
HAVE TO SEE
THE WHOLE
STAIRCASE, JUST
*take the
first step.*

Martin Luther King Jr

YOU ARE NEVER TOO OLD TO SET ANOTHER GOAL OR TO DREAM A NEW DREAM.

LES BROWN

YOU CAN
TOTALLY
DO THIS

If you're interested in finding out more about our books, find us on Facebook at *Summersdale Publishers* and follow us on Twitter at *@Summersdale*.

www.summersdale.com

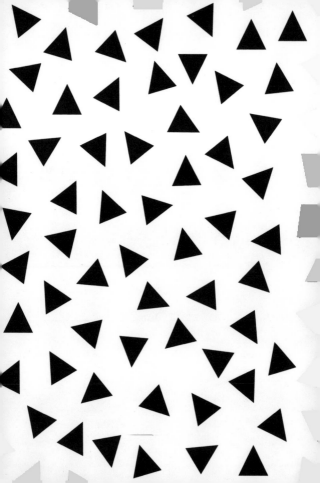